Sexual Reflections:
A Workbook for
Designing and Celebrating
Your Sexual Health Plan

© 2018 Alexandra Katehakis
All rights reserved. This book or any portion thereof may not be reproduced or used in any manner whatsoever without the express written permission of the publisher except for the use of brief quotations in a book review or similar work.

Printed in USA
First Printing, 2018
ISBN 978-1717166128

Designed by Ellison / Goodreau
Edited by Alisa Reich
Art by Terry Marks-Tarlow

Published by
Alexandra Katehakis, Ph.D.
Los Angeles CA 90025
(310) 801-9574

Sexual Reflections:

A Workbook for Designing and Celebrating Your Sexual Health Plan

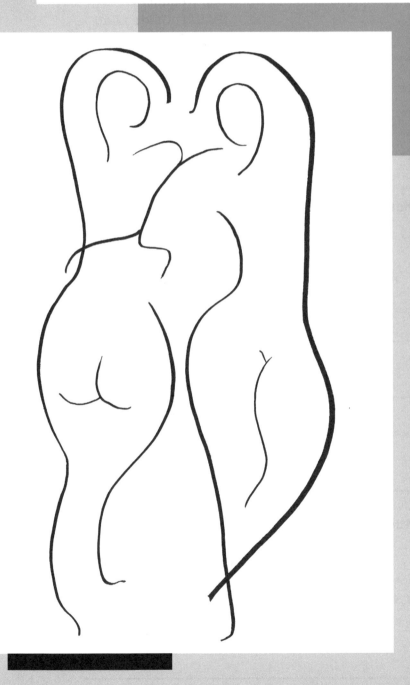

Alexandra Katehakis, Ph.D.

Table of Contents

Welcome		7
Chapter 1	Psychobiological Approach to Sex Addiction Treatment	9
	(PASAT) Guide	10
	I. Tracking	10
	II. Bodily-Based Transference and Countertransference	11
	III. Resources	11
	IV. Present Awareness	11
	V. Finishing	
Chapter 2	**Katehakis Integrative Sex Therapy**	
	KIST Model:	13
	Individually-Based Criteria of Healthy Sexuality	
	I. Physical Dimension	15
	II. Affective Dimension	15
	III. Cognitive Dimension	15
	IV. Interpersonal-Intrapsychic Dimension	15
	V. Spiritual Dimension	15
Chapter 3	Using this Workbook	17
Chapter 4	The Physical Dimension of Sexuality	21
	I. Your Sexual Health	22
	II. Your Sexual Anatomy	31
Chapter 5	The Affective and Cognitive Dimensions of Sexuality	41
	I. List of Addictive or Problematic Sexual Behaviors	42
	II. List of Personal Values	49
	III. List of Sexual Values	57
	IV. List of Preferred Sex Acts	66
	V. Preferred Sex Acts or a Repetition of Your Trauma?	74
	VI. Watch and Wait List	82
	VII. Your Sexual Health Plan (SHP)	90

Chapter 6	The Interpersonal-Intrapsychic Dimension of Sexuality	97
	I. Discussion for the Partnered	98
	II. Dating Plan for the Single	102
Chapter 7	The Spiritual Dimension of Sexuality	115
	Your Sexual Health Checklist	126
	Farewell	129
	Additional Notes	130

Appendix THERAPIST ANNOTATIONS 133

Chapter 1
Psychobiological Approach to Sex Addiction Treatment
(PASAT) Guide i
I. Tracking ii
II. Tracking Gestures (therapist information)
III. Somatic Countertransference iii
IV. Titration
V. Completion of the Response iv
VI. Resources v
VII. Present Awareness vi
VIII. Regulation of Dorsal Motor Vagal Responses vii
IX. Pendulation viii
X. Finishing ix

Chapter 5
V. Preferred Sex Acts or a Repetition of Your Trauma? x

Chapter 6
Guided Meditation — Therapist Script xi

Welcome

Congratulations on making it to this point in your recovery! Sexual addiction is a syndrome that manifests in destructive, often painful sexual behaviors. It's born of severe distress in early childhood due to neglect or to emotional, physical, or sexual abuse. This early abuse injures the growing human attachment system–our main source of emotional support and resilience–and makes it go haywire in search of some external substance or act (like sex) for comfort. As you well know, stopping problematic sexual behaviors is no easy feat. But once you've done it, life starts to feel totally different, as actual *choices* about where, when, how, and with whom you have sex become available again—and for some, for the first time.

And even if you don't identify as a sex addict, but have engaged in problematic sexual behaviors (such as an affair or excessive Internet pornography viewing), this workbook is designed to help you create a Sexual Health Plan (SHP) that reflects how *you* want to design your sex life. You will be guided by your therapist through simple, but sometimes challenging, processes that teach you to listen to the impulses in your body to learn what's right for you sexually at this point in time. Be on the lookout for the impulsive part of you that wants to green-light everything; Instead, let your heart and your body guide you to your truth. For even if both strategies lead you to the same sex act, listening to your heart and your body will bring you there with a free and fully conscious intention.

As you travel this road, keep an open mind and remove all restrictions, all the "should's," from the conversation. Be courageous in your rigorous honesty with yourself. Remember, this plan discovers *your* deepest, truest desires. Finding them is a process, so change and growth go with the territory as you work through the book.

Most of all, be creative, play and have fun!

— **Alexandra Katehakis**

NOTE TO THERAPISTS

In chapters 1, 5 and 6 you will be directed to the Appendix in the back of this workbook. There you will find Therapist Annotations that will assist you in guiding your client through the corresponding clinical processes in this workbook.

Chapter 1

Psychobiological Approach to Sex Addiction Treatment (PASAT) Guide

THERAPISTS:
See Appendix pages i – ix

This workbook relies on the Psychobiological Approach to Sex Addiction Treatment (PASAT) Guide to help you discover what's true for you. It may take a session or two to read through this guide with your therapist, but don't skip this process or your results will fall short.

PASAT centers on the relationship between you and your therapist and the felt experiences you will have shared. You'll be asked often to notice the feelings, impulses and sensations in your body, record or reflect on them using worksheets, and discuss them with your therapist. This way of working familiarizes you with how your nervous system responds to a stimulus. By getting to know your body/mind in this way, you'll learn more accurately what feels sexually healthy and pleasurable to you, and what doesn't. This process will also help you become less compartmentalized about your sexuality–less cut-off from your self when you think about or have sex. In other words, there's no place for secrets about your sexual preferences in this work, only honesty about what brings you sexual fulfillment and how your therapist can assist you in making those acts part of your sexual life.

The user-friendly PASAT guide that follows will help you track the inner landscape of your body/mind. Its steps are: Tracking, Bodily-Based Transference and Countertransference, Resources, Present Awareness, and Finishing.

I. Tracking

Tracking means paying close attention to sensations and impulses in your body. Get into the habit of tracking your bodily-based sensations as they arise while you talk about the various workbook assignments and about other issues with your therapist.

Your therapist will also be tracking the physiological changes he or she sees in you, and will ask you about them.

You will be invited to give words, without too much thinking, to the sensations and impulses in your body. Your therapist may ask a body part to "speak," and you can just jump in and say whatever comes to mind. You'll be encouraged to use descriptors that emerge in the moment, such as colors or an image that captures your inner experience ("My heart feels black" or "I feel butterflies in my stomach"). Your therapist may ask you to narrate your shifting internal experiences, without judgment, as they occur. For example, if you say, "I feel stuck," your therapist may ask, "Where are you feeling stuck in your body?" Do the best you can to answer from your body and not your mind.

Your therapist will also raise your awareness of your gestures or movements. These nonverbal communications range from expressions of anger (e.g., clenched fists) to self-soothing (e.g., a hand on the chest). Your therapist will ask you about these gestures in service of gently bringing your awareness into the present moment.

II. Bodily-Based Transference and Countertransference

There will undoubtedly be times when you notice feelings toward your therapist as you negotiate the nooks and crannies of your sexual psyche. You may feel frustrated, embarrassed, or even sexually attracted to him or her, regardless of your sexual orientation. These are normal feelings of what's called "transference" in psychotherapeutic language, because we all transfer, or infuse, our feelings into a person we're close with. It's natural that your therapist might become the object of your anger at having to be in recovery, or the object of your sexual fantasy because you're talking about sex and sexuality with him or her. Don't despair! This is a common, healthy, and useful experience when in therapy, and the best response is to talk about it. Whatever feelings come up for you in this therapeutic work can help you clarify who you are sexually, so remember to take risks by being rigorously honest.

Throughout this process, your therapist will also be reporting his or her experience of what it feels like to be in your presence (countertransference). Like you, he or she will track the impulses in his or her body, and tell you what he or she is noticing when the information would be helpful to you.

For example, let's say you report feeling "blank." The therapist will pay close attention to what he or she is feeling in his or her own body, and may reply with something like, "I, too, am noticing a blankness in the middle of my body." Even in casual conversation, people often verbalize their bodily feelings in the presence of others. The difference now is that you and your therapist will talk about these sensations in a way that increases your ability to see yourself and to be seen, known, and understood by another.

III. Resources

There will be times when you feel like you're getting too anxious or even shutting down. If this happens, your therapist will guide you to use a simple inner *resource* you already have: the thought or memory of anyone or anything that brings you into a physical state of calm.

For example, your resource may be:
a. A safe place
b. An experience in which you found comfort and connection with another person or with nature
c. A secure, calming presence (grandparent, special teacher, pet, favorite object)
d. A life experience in which you were victorious (escaped a difficult situation, climbed a mountain, or accomplished something you thought was impossible)

Remember to trust the process and that your therapist can guide you out of any discomfort.

IV. Present Awareness

There may be times when your therapist brings your awareness into the present moment. He or she may ask you to ground or connect deeply to the Earth by simply noticing your feet on the floor, the weight of your body on the chair, objects in the environment, scenes outside the window, or smells that bring you into the present field. This well-known mindfulness practice can focus and soothe you no matter where you are.

V. Finishing

It's important to bring every session to a close, especially if you're dealing with traumatic issues. So your therapist may ask if you're "finished" after a particularly emotional session. She or he will check in with you about how you're feeling in the moment. Your therapist may also suggest you simply take some deep breaths right then, or take a walk around the block before you drive off. Any way you make it happen, it's a good idea to bring yourself back into your body and the present before you go on to the next activity in your life.

Chapter 2

KIST Model: Individually-Based Criteria of Healthy Sexuality

The field of sex addiction therapy has come a long way since its inception in 1983, when "sexual recovery" meant simply abstaining from sexually harmful behaviors. This workbook transcends even its updated, sexual sustainability-based program by creating a model to help you, the recovering person, achieve not just non-compulsive sexuality, but *optimal sexuality*, and to help you achieve it through your own self-agency. To do that, the Katehakis Integrative Sex Therapy (KIST) Model offers specific actions that support, first, abstinence from destructive sexual behaviors and, ultimately, engagement in healthy sexual behaviors that you choose and which lead you toward optimal sexual experiences.

The KIST Model applies the World Health Organization (WHO) 2006 definition of sexual health:
> Sexual health is a state of physical, emotional, mental and social well-being; it is not merely the absence of disease, dysfunction, or infirmity. Sexual health requires a positive and respectful approach to sexuality and sexual relationships, as well as the possibility of having pleasurable and safe sexual experiences free of coercion, discrimination, and violence. For sexual health to be attained and maintained, the sexual rights of all persons must be respected, protected and fulfilled (p. 5).

Building on the WHO approach to sexual health, the KIST Model defines *healthy sexuality* as *any consensual sexual act with yourself or an adult(s) that you and your therapist agree is healthy, based on how it impacts your physical, emotional, mental, social, and spiritual well-being*. That is, the KIST Model explains, and sees as blended, five dimensions of sexuality in each individual: physical, affective, cognitive, interpersonal-intrapsychic, and spiritual.

Whether you're aiming to repair your relationship after an affair, are recovering from childhood sexual abuse, or identify as a recovering sex addict, you will be using the following cognitive (knowing-based) and affective (feeling-based) guide in your quest for healthy sex. Keep in mind that all of the five dimensions operate together and simultaneously, and that each one of them-not just the physical dimension—manifests in the body. As you complete the work in this book, you'll be able, literally, to check off items in its list of tasks and criteria for all five dimensions of sexuality, and discuss each with your therapist. But for now, all you have to do is read this section and consider it a roadmap for what you will accomplish. Let's take a look.

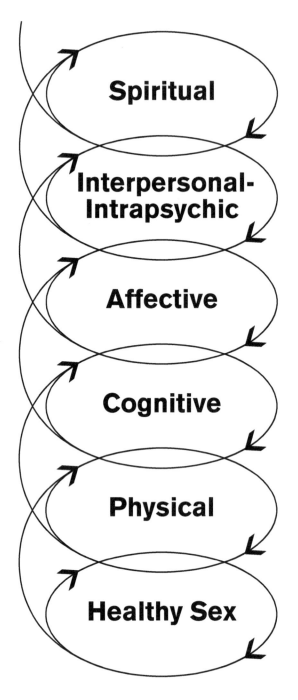

Katehakis Integrative Sex Therapy (KIST) Model
Founded on healthy sexuality, the Katehakis Integrative Sex Therapy (KIST) Model takes you through all of these dimensions, each one of which includes and transcends the previous one.

Individually-Based Criteria for Five Dimensions of Healthy Sexuality

I. Physical Dimension
a. You can distinguish sexual behaviors that are harmful or exploitative to yourself or to another from sexual behaviors that bring dignity, vitality, and pleasure to yourself and to another.
b. You are aware of your sexual response cycle, and enjoy satisfactory physical responsiveness based on optimal functioning in your brain/body/mind.
c. You understand your sexual body (anatomy, physiology, sexual dysfunction and related needs), and have gotten tested for STIs and other physical risks.

II. Affective Dimension
a. You don't feel guilty or shameful about sex and sexual behavior and you don't reenact previous trauma that induces dissociative feelings (loss of or distancing from your self).
b. You can track and name the impulses in your body as emotions, and can trust these impulses as a personal guide to what feels right and what feels wrong to you.
c. You can communicate and receive communication about thoughts and feelings, and possess the potential for intimacy, vulnerability, and a long-term love relationship.
d. You are excited about sex and feel that pleasurable sexual acts restore your sense of dignity and worth.

III. Cognitive Dimension
a. You can relate to a lover with appropriate boundaries: Specifically, you know when to say "no;" can hear "no" from another; don't violate your dignity or body by engaging in unwanted sexual experiences; and don't take sexual advantage of another through physical or psychological manipulation.
b. If you're single, you have constructed a dating plan and a sexual plan; if you're in a relationship, you have constructed a sexual plan.
c. You can take deliberate actions to set the stage for the kind of sexual experience you want.

IV. Interpersonal-Intrapsychic Dimension
a. You have comfortably talked with a partner about a range of preferred sexual experiences and have disclosed to a partner your health status (HIV, STI, activity in or recovery from sex addiction, alcoholism, gambling or other addictions).
b. You report comfort with a range of preferred sexual experiences, including masturbation, and you can discuss them with a partner, friend, potential love interest, and therapist without shame.
c. You experience and can report to your therapist openness to discovering your personal truth via the senses during sex.
d. You have a felt sense in your body that sexual preferences and choices are congruent with your gender identity.

V. Spiritual Dimension
a. You have made a conscious choice about your spiritual or religious preferences (including agnosticism or atheism) through your chosen avenues (12-step program, teacher, mentor, clergy person, or therapist), and you can discuss your choices with your therapist and your partner.
b. Spiritual or religious beliefs enrich your sexual experience rather than provoke shame or guilt.
c. You remain fluid during sex, can make a meaningful connection between the spiritual and the sexual, and can choose to process spiritual/sexual experiences with another to understand and deepen your sexual/spiritual life.

Addictive Sex	Healthy Sex
Originates from a shame-based sexuality	**Deepens a sense of self and embraces one's erotic, animal nature**
Takes advantage of others	**Is mutually respectful and honoring**
Compromises one's integrity	**Reinforces a congruent sense of self**
Confuses intensity for intimacy	**Recognizes vulnerability as the road to intimacy and eroticism**
Reenacts trauma and cements old arousal patterns in the brain	**Allows for exploration, sexual meaning making, and "rewiring" the brain**
Requires some pathological dissociation (distance from self)	**Requires a person to experience the feelings in her or his body**
Is fixated on the past and future, usually inaccurately idealized	**Demands experiencing the present and staying relational**
Relies on self-loathing and self-destruction	**Relies on self-love and nurturance**
Is about power and control over another	**Is about surrender and vulnerability with another**
Is covert and manipulative	**Is direct and requires risk-taking**
Serves to avoid feelings at all costs	**Requires willingness to feel deeply**
Is fraudulent	**Creates congruence**
Creates tolerance (always requires more stimulation)	**Requires self-confrontation for growth**
Requires compartmentalization	**Demands truth and authenticity**
Is rigid and routine	**Is fluid; celebrates life, variety, partnership, and one's spirituality**
Is without meaning, eroticism, or a spiritual connection	**Makes meaning and embraces one's erotic self as a pathway to spirituality**

Note: Adapted [with permission] from *Don't Call It Love*, by Patrick Carnes, 1991; Reprinted with permission from *Erotic Intelligence*, by Alexandra Katehakis, 2010.

Chapter 3

Using this Workbook

Congratulations, again! You have reached a point in your sexual recovery where you and your therapist have decided that you're ready to define your personally preferred, optimal Sexual Health Plan (SHP).

This process should occur in session with your therapist or with a support/process group and a therapist present. It may take many sessions before you accurately discern what optimal sex means to you. Often in the sexual recovery process, many voices chime in on what's okay and what isn't. Your partner, sponsor, fellows in recovery, friends, the popular culture, and even your therapist all have opinions about your sex life. But this is the time to be honest with yourself about what a healthy, pleasurable sex life *for you* would include. So take the risk of talking about even sexual acts you feel are taboo; by the end of this process you will have clarity about what supports your sexual recovery, what doesn't, and what *you* need and want in your sex life.

As you work through each section below, expect that your nervous system will get activated or "triggered." That's how your body will guide you to your truth, so let it. When these feelings arise, report them to your therapist, scaling them from 1(if you feel little to no activation in your body) to 10 (if you're feeling a maximum amount of activation in your body). With your therapist's help, you'll soon be able to notice whether your activation feels like an aroused, excited state (fast heartbeat, sweaty palms, sexual arousal) or a shame state (a "red hot" sensation originating in your gut, sometimes with flushed neck and face).

Activation Scale

10
9
8
7
6
5
4
3
2
1

At the end of every section in the workbook you'll be asked to find and scale your activation and to fill in a Somatic Notes worksheet, so you get into the habit of tracking the impulses in your body. This practice will help you get used to paying attention to sensations in your body when looking for your truth, rather than relying solely on your thoughts.

The Activation Scale is shown to the left.

To use it, gently turn your attention to the sensations in your body so you can report where in your body you're feeling activated. If you have difficulty verbalizing where the sensation is occurring, use the Somatic Notes worksheet as a useful prompt. Doing so will help you get acquainted with the impulses and sensations in your body, locate them, and listen to your feelings even before you listen to your thoughts.

You'll also see the heading, "Homework." After you complete a section in the workbook, you'll be asked to do some homework related to a drawing that accompanies that section, and then to reflect on it fully. Experiencing evocative images and responding with your own words will deepen your take-away of each step in the process, and prepare you to move on to the next.

It's highly recommended that you color in each drawing so that you bring it to life through some of the most authentic parts of yourself: your imagination and your intuition. Viewing each drawing, and especially coloring it in, will help elicit an image or memory that you're asked to write a story or poem about. Reconstructing your past by using your imagination to tell a story or a poem based on what the drawing brings up for you lets you learn more about yourself on an intuitive, emotional level.

Begin your writing with a statement such as, "I remember a time when…" or "Once upon a time…" or be creative in your poetry. Whatever you choose to write, create a beginning and ending to your tale, and include how you felt or feel. Let your imagination run wild. Don't censor yourself. Allow your creative imagination and intuition their full bloom.

After you write, dig deep. Ask yourself, "What's the clearest part of the image, memory, story or poem?" "What's the strongest emotion coming up for me when I look at or color the drawing?" "Do I associate a specific action with the drawing?" "How old do I imagine myself as being in the memory, story or poem?" After you process your reactions with your therapist, ask yourself, "Is there any part of the memory, story or poem I'd like to rewrite?"

Chapter 4

The Physical Dimension of Sexuality

In this session, your therapist will ask you a series of questions about your sexual health, below. Write down your answers so the two of you can process them and consider what actions you'd like to take.

I. Your Sexual Health

a. Have you been tested for STIs and HIV?

b. What were the results? Write about your feelings before, during and after testing when you received your results.

c. Do you think you have infected anyone? How do you feel about that?

d. If so, whom have you infected, and have you told the person/s?

e. How do you feel about telling the person/s?

f. Will you tell the person/s you infected? If "yes," what will you say? If "no," why not?

g. When you think about talking to someone you may have infected, are you aware of any feelings that arise?

h. If so, what are they?

i. Can you imagine having a conversation about the STIs you've contracted with your partner, or with a new partner if you're single?

j. After answering these questions aloud, can you talk comfortably with a partner about your sexual history, recovery from sex addiction, alcoholism, gambling or any other addiction? If not, why not? What else do you have to attend to in order to feel comfortable with your sexual history?

_____
_____
_____
_____
_____
_____
_____
_____
_____
_____
_____
_____
_____
_____

Activation Scale

10
9
8
7
6
5
4
3
2
1

Are you aware of any feelings arising as we talk about this topic? If so, what are they?

Process any feelings or thoughts that arise. Use the Activation Scale to indicate how activated you are. Notice emotions evoked in your body, and indicate those on the Somatic Notes worksheet if it's helpful.

Somatic Notes

Facial Cues
(I notice tension in my jaw, around my lips, between my eyes, forehead, etc.)

Bodily Cues
(I notice tension in my arms, legs, chest, stomach, rectum, etc. I notice that I'm fidgeting, have shallow breathing, or I'm not breathing, have a dry mouth, etc.)

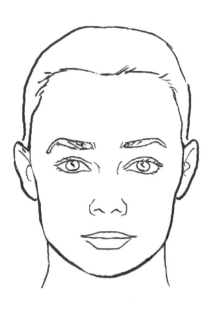

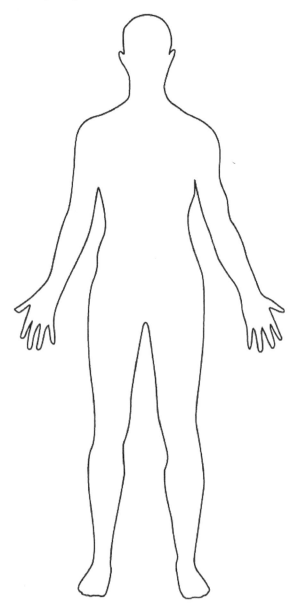

Vocal Cues
(I notice constriction in my throat, my voice seems different, my tone of voice is higher or lower, etc.)

_____
_____
_____
_____
_____
_____
_____

Behavioral Cues
(I'm having difficulty concentrating, etc.)

_____
_____
_____
_____
_____
_____
_____
_____

Homework

Color in the image on the following page. →

Then, write a story or poem about the image, or a memory it brings up for you. Remember to create a beginning and ending and to acknowledge any feelings the image evoked in you.

My Story / Poem / Memory

Reflections Log

Use this space between sessions to record any thoughts, feelings, images, memories or ideas that came to you as you completed this section.

II. Your Sexual Anatomy

a. Write about how well you understand your genital functioning. Is there anything you would like to know more about? If so, what?

b. How do you feel about your body? Do you like or dislike it? What do you like or dislike? Write about your feelings about specific body parts such as hands, feet, legs, chest/breasts, or qualities, such as height, weight, and so forth.

c. How do you feel about your genitals? Do you like or dislike them? What do you like or dislike about them?

d. How well do you understand your sexual arousal cycle? Describe what you know.

e. Do you know what you need sexually to have an orgasm? Can you communicate that to a partner? If not, what would make it easier for you to do so?

f. Do you know what kind of touch you like (e.g., soft, rough, tender, firm)? Where on your body or genitals do you like to be touched? Is there a shape, rhythm, or pattern of touch you prefer?

g. Males: Do you struggle with any sexual dysfunction issues that need to be addressed (erectile dysfunction, premature ejaculation, a medical condition)? Have you seen a urologist for these issues? If so, what was the outcome of that meeting? If not, why not? When will you do so?

h. Females: Do you struggle with any sexual dysfunction issues that need to be addressed (pelvic pain disorders, anorgasmia, a medical condition)? Have you seen a gynecologist for these issues? If so, what was the outcome of that meeting? If not, why not? When will you do so?

i. What more would you like to understand about your body or your sexual arousal cycle?

j. Can you imagine having a conversation with your partner, or with a new partner if you're single, about the previous questions? How activated do you get when you think about that conversation?

_____
_____
_____
_____
_____
_____
_____
_____
_____
_____
_____
_____
_____

Activation Scale

10
9
8
7
6
5
4
3
2
1

Are you aware of any feelings arising as we talk about this topic? If so, what are they?

Process any feelings or thoughts that arise. Use the Activation Scale to indicate how activated you are. Notice emotions evoked in your body, and indicate those on the Somatic Notes worksheet if it's helpful.

Somatic Notes

Facial Cues
(I notice tension in my jaw, around my lips, between my eyes, forehead, etc.)

Bodily Cues
(I notice tension in my arms, legs, chest, stomach, rectum, etc. I notice that I'm fidgeting, have shallow breathing, or I'm not breathing, have a dry mouth, etc.)

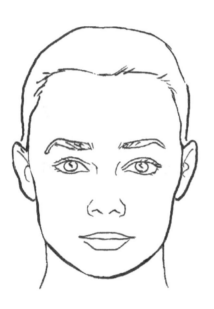

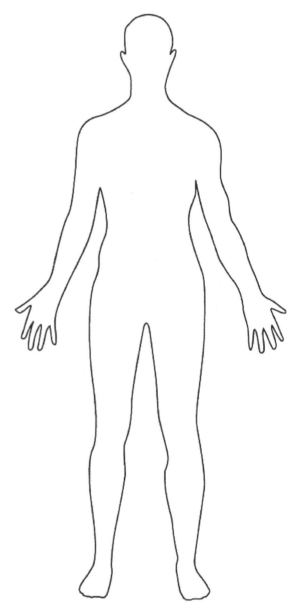

Vocal Cues
(I notice constriction in my throat, my voice seems different, my tone of voice is higher or lower, etc.)

_____
_____
_____
_____
_____
_____
_____

Behavioral Cues
(I'm having difficulty concentrating, etc.)

_____
_____
_____
_____
_____
_____
_____

Homework

Color in the image on the following page. →

Then, write a story or poem about the image, or a memory it brings up for you. Remember to create a beginning and ending and to acknowledge any feelings the image evoked in you.

My Story / Poem / Memory

Reflections Log

Use this space between sessions to record any thoughts, feelings, images, memories or ideas that came to you as you completed this section.

Chapter 5

The Affective and Cognitive Dimensions of Sexuality

THERAPISTS:
See Appendix page x

This phase of the process is designed to assist you in comfortably talking with a partner about a range of preferred sexual experiences including your disclosures about your sexual health status, your sexual preferences, feelings, and choices you've made with your therapist that are congruent with your gender identity and how you feel about your sexuality.

I. List of Addictive or Problematic Sexual Behaviors

Make a list of sexual behaviors that are harmful or exploitative to yourself or others. This would include your "acting out," "bottom line," or "inner circle" behaviors. Be specific and detailed.

Read the list on the following page aloud to your therapist. Process any feelings or thoughts that arise. Use the Activation Scale to indicate how activated you are. Write the scaling number in the right column next to each behavior. Notice emotions evoked in your body, and indicate those on the Somatic Notes worksheet if it's helpful.

Activation Scale

10
9
8
7
6
5
4
3
2
1

1.	

2.	

3.	

4.	

5.	

6.	

Somatic Notes

Facial Cues
(I notice tension in my jaw, around my lips, between my eyes, forehead, etc.)

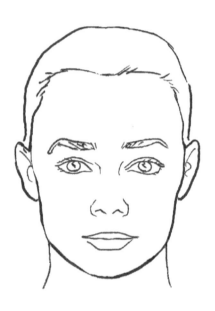

Bodily Cues
(I notice tension in my arms, legs, chest, stomach, rectum, etc. I notice that I'm fidgeting, have shallow breathing, or I'm not breathing, have a dry mouth, etc.)

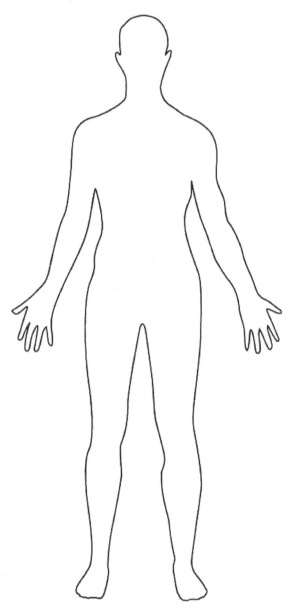

Vocal Cues
(I notice constriction in my throat, my voice seems different, my tone of voice is higher or lower, etc.)

_____

_____

_____

_____

_____

_____

_____

Behavioral Cues
(I'm having difficulty concentrating, etc.)

_____

_____

_____

_____

_____

_____

_____

Homework

Color in the image on the following page. →

Then, write a story or poem about the image, or a memory it brings up for you. Remember to create a beginning and ending and to acknowledge any feelings the image evoked in you.

My Story / Poem / Memory

Reflections Log

Use this space between sessions to record any thoughts, feelings, images, memories or ideas that came to you as you completed this section.

II. List of Personal Values

Adventure	**Mastery**	**Religion**	**Joy**	**Authenticity**
Success	**Loyalty**	**Aesthetics**	**Purpose**	**Forgiveness**
Play	**Honesty**	**Commitment**	**Creativity**	**Principles**
Respect	**Fidelity**	**Directness**	**Non-traditional**	**Education**
Risk	**Compassion**	**Stability**	**Spirituality**	**Health**
Intimacy	**Intelligence**	**Tradition**	**Vulnerability**	**Humor**
Vitality	**Trust**	**Monogamy**	**Well-Being**	**Empathy**
Curiosity	**Awareness**	**Moderation**	**Honor**	**Freedom**

Circle up to ten words that best specify your Personal Values.

Number the top six values you would like to be present in your sex life, in order of importance (1 = most important; 6 = least important).

Activation Scale

10
9
8
7
6
5
4
3
2
1

Next, define exactly what your six top values mean to you, writing one sentence for each. For example, "Authenticity means I feel safe being myself in all my relationships," or "Directness means I can speak my mind and hear the same from others."

Read your Personal Values and their meanings aloud to your therapist. Track and scale your emotions as you do so, and write the scaling number in the right column next to each Personal Value. Notice the emotions your values evoke in your body, and indicate those on the Somatic Notes worksheet if it's helpful.

1.

2.

3.

4.

5.

6.

Somatic Notes

Facial Cues
(I notice tension in my jaw, around my lips, between my eyes, forehead, etc.)

Bodily Cues
(I notice tension in my arms, legs, chest, stomach, rectum, etc. I notice that I'm fidgeting, have shallow breathing, or I'm not breathing, have a dry mouth, etc.)

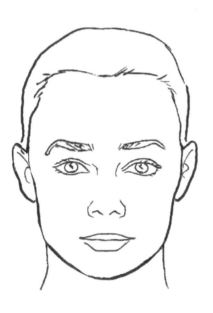

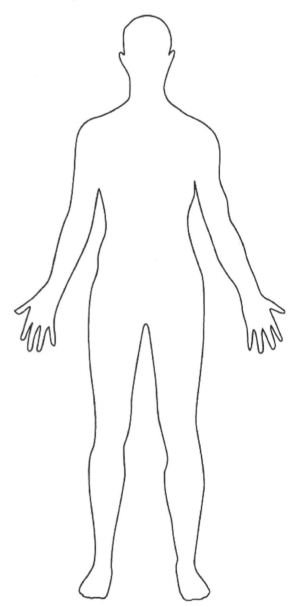

Vocal Cues
(I notice constriction in my throat, my voice seems different, my tone of voice is higher or lower, etc.)

_____
_____
_____
_____
_____
_____
_____
_____

Behavioral Cues
(I'm having difficulty concentrating, etc.)

_____
_____
_____
_____
_____
_____
_____
_____

Homework

Color in the image on the following page. →

Then, write a story or poem about the image, or a memory it brings up for you. Remember to create a beginning and ending and to acknowledge any feelings the image evoked in you.

My Story / Poem / Memory

Reflections Log

Use this space between sessions to record any thoughts, feelings, images, memories or ideas that came to you as you completed this section.

III. List of Sexual Values

Intimate	Raunchy	Pain	Joy	Erotic
Aphrodisiacs	Loyalty	Beauty	Lust	Nurturing
Play	Vulnerability	Touch	Creativity	Power
Spirituality	Domination	Sensuality	Privacy	Desire
Risky	Romance	Wild Abandon	Fantasy	Flirtatious
Freedom	Emotion	Nasty	Animalistic	Pleasure
Vitality	Trust	Caressing	Ritualistic	Resilience
Submission	Objectification	Moderation	Foreplay	BDSM

Circle up to ten words that best specify your Sexual Values / Turn-Ons.

Number the top six values you would like to be present in your sex life, in order of importance (1 = most important; 6 = least important).

Activation Scale

10
9
8
7
6
5
4
3
2
1

Next, define exactly what your six top values mean to you, writing one sentence for each. For example, "Pleasure means I can be open to my partner about the importance of giving and receiving pleasure the way I like it," or "Wild abandon means I can reveal myself in wildly sexual ways without judgment from my partner."

Read your Sexual Values and their meanings aloud to your therapist. Track and scale your emotions as you do so, then write the scaling number in the right column next to each Sexual Value. Notice and report the emotions your values evoke in your body, and indicate those on the Somatic Notes worksheet if it's helpful.

1.	

2.	

3.	

4.	

5.	

6.	

Somatic Notes

Facial Cues
(I notice tension in my jaw, around my lips, between my eyes, forehead, etc.)

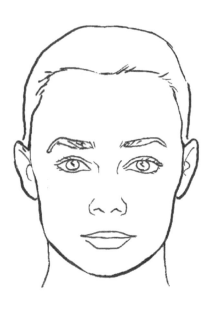

Bodily Cues
(I notice tension in my arms, legs, chest, stomach, rectum, etc. I notice that I'm fidgeting, have shallow breathing, or I'm not breathing, have a dry mouth, etc.)

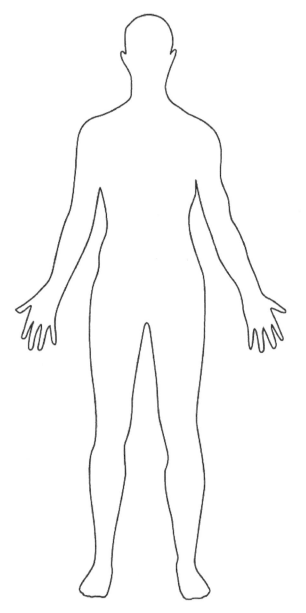

Vocal Cues
(I notice constriction in my throat, my voice seems different, my tone of voice is higher or lower, etc.)

_____

_____

_____

_____

_____

_____

Behavioral Cues
(I'm having difficulty concentrating, etc.)

_____

_____

_____

_____

_____

_____

Homework

Color in the image on the following page. →

Then, write a story or poem about the image, or a memory it brings up for you. Remember to create a beginning and ending and to acknowledge any feelings the image evoked in you.

My Story / Poem / Memory

Reflections Log

Use this space between sessions to record any thoughts, feelings, images, memories or ideas that came to you as you completed this section.

IV. List of Preferred Sex Acts

Activation Scale

10
9
8
7
6
5
4
3
2
1

Make a list of the sex acts you enjoy or ones you haven't tried but think you would like to. Perhaps you engaged in these acts during your infidelity or addiction, or have seen them while looking at pornography. Give yourself permission to be honest about what's sexually arousing and pleasurable to you without judgment, and include what you value sexually from page 57. For example, "I value freedom in my sex life so trying multiple positions is arousing to me," OR "Being submissive during sex was pleasurable to me during my addiction, so I would like to try this with my partner."

Read your Preferred Sex Acts aloud to your therapist, one at a time. Track and scale your emotions as you do so, and write the scaling number in the right column next to each Preferred Sex Act. Notice and track the emotions each of your Preferred Sex Acts evokes in your body, and indicate those on the Somatic Notes worksheet if it's helpful.

1.

2.

3.

4.

5.

6.

Somatic Notes

Facial Cues
(I notice tension in my jaw, around my lips, between my eyes, forehead, etc.)

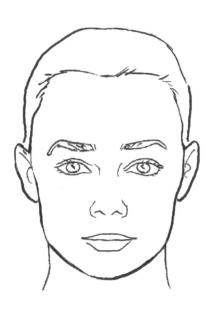

Bodily Cues
(I notice tension in my arms, legs, chest, stomach, rectum, etc. I notice that I'm fidgeting, have shallow breathing, or I'm not breathing, have a dry mouth, etc.)

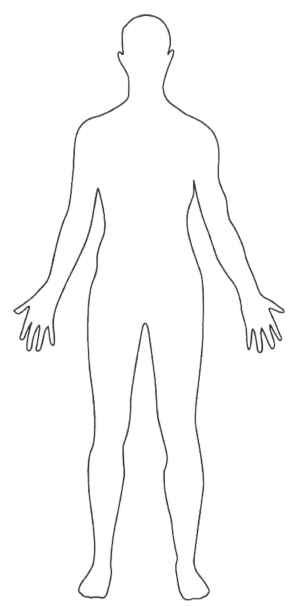

Vocal Cues
(I notice constriction in my throat, my voice seems different, my tone of voice is higher or lower, etc.)

_____

_____

_____

_____

_____

_____

_____

Behavioral Cues
(I'm having difficulty concentrating, etc.)

_____

_____

_____

_____

_____

_____

_____

Homework

Color in the image on the following page. →

Then, write a story or poem about the image, or a memory it brings up for you. Remember to create a beginning and ending and to acknowledge any feelings the image evoked in you.

My Story / Poem / Memory

Reflections Log

Use this space between sessions to record any thoughts, feelings, images, memories or ideas that came to you as you completed this section.

V. Preferred Sex Acts or a Repetition of Your Trauma?

Activation Scale

10
9
8
7
6
5
4
3
2
1

Go back and look at your List of Preferred Sex Acts on page 67, summarize them in one or two words, and write them on the following page.

Next, say each sex act aloud, then notice what you're feeling in your body and where you're feeling it. Indicate the emotions on the Somatic Notes worksheet and write the scaling number in the right column next to the sex act. This is the time to determine whether you're feeling bodily-based arousal or shame about the sex act. Can you make the distinction? If not, ask your therapist to assist you in the exploration.

If you are feeling shame, take this time to process all Preferred Sex Acts to determine whether the shame is related to untreated trauma or to your judgment about the sex act being "dirty" or "wrong." Your therapist will assist you by asking some specific questions.

1.

2.

3.

4.

5.

6.

Somatic Notes

Facial Cues
(I notice tension in my jaw, around my lips, between my eyes, forehead, etc.)

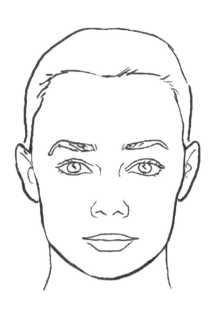

Bodily Cues
(I notice tension in my arms, legs, chest, stomach, rectum, etc. I notice that I'm fidgeting, have shallow breathing, or I'm not breathing, have a dry mouth, etc.)

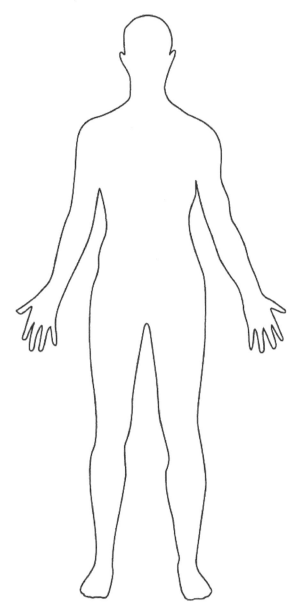

Homework

Vocal Cues
(I notice constriction in my throat, my voice seems different, my tone of voice is higher or lower, etc.)

_____
_____
_____
_____
_____
_____
_____

Behavioral Cues
(I'm having difficulty concentrating, etc.)

_____
_____
_____
_____
_____
_____
_____
_____

Color in the image on the following page. →

Then, write a story or poem about the image, or a memory it brings up for you. Remember to create a beginning and ending and to acknowledge any feelings the image evoked in you.

My Story / Poem / Memory

Reflections Log

Use this space between sessions to record any thoughts, feelings, images, memories or ideas that came to you as you completed this section.

VI. Watch and Wait List

Activation Scale

- 10
- 9
- 8
- 7
- 6
- 5
- 4
- 3
- 2
- 1

If you felt toxic/addictive shame or were disturbed by one or more of your preferred sex acts on page 67, you will have processed your feelings with your therapist by now. Is any sex act on your List of Preferred Sex Acts a reenactment of unresolved trauma? Check the sex acts on your preferred list to see if they violate any ideal on your List of Personal Values on page 49. If the sex act reenacts unresolved sexual trauma or violates your personal values, then it doesn't belong on your SHP at this time. It is recommended that you do some specific trauma work to resolve lingering issues.

List those sex acts that reenact trauma or violate your personal values (and therefore do not belong on your SHP) on your Watch and Wait list, here.

Look over your Watch and Wait list. Does it seem right to you at this time? If so, notice how you feel about each item on the list by scaling your activation and tracking your feelings. Note that you might feel sadness or loss from putting a sex act on this list, even though you think it's the best thing for your emotional sobriety at this time. But remember, this is a Watch and Wait list just for now, not a permanent declaration of abstinence from these sex acts.

1.	

2.	

3.	

4.	

5.	

6.	

Somatic Notes

Facial Cues
(I notice tension in my jaw, around my lips, between my eyes, forehead, etc.)

Bodily Cues
(I notice tension in my arms, legs, chest, stomach, rectum, etc. I notice that I'm fidgeting, have shallow breathing, or I'm not breathing, have a dry mouth, etc.)

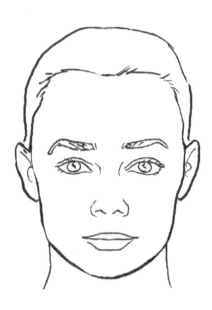

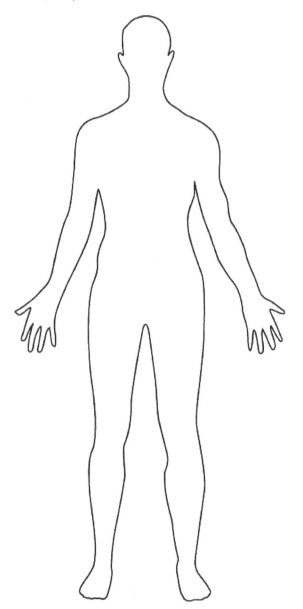

Vocal Cues
(I notice constriction in my throat, my voice seems different, my tone of voice is higher or lower, etc.)

_____

_____

_____

_____

_____

_____

_____

Behavioral Cues
(I'm having difficulty concentrating, etc.)

_____

_____

_____

_____

_____

_____

_____

Homework

Color in the image on the following page. →

Then, write a story or poem about the image, or a memory it brings up for you. Remember to create a beginning and ending and to acknowledge any feelings the image evoked in you.

My Story / Poem / Memory

Reflections Log

Use this space between sessions to record any thoughts, feelings, images, memories or ideas that came to you as you completed this section.

VII. Your Sexual Health Plan (SHP)

List your Preferred Sex Acts that do not evoke unhealthy or toxic shame in you. If you're aroused by the idea of a sex act and it doesn't reenact trauma or violate your Personal Values, list it as an SHP Preferred Sex Act.

Read each of these listed SHP Preferred Sex Acts aloud one more time, then track and scale your emotions. Write the scaling number in the right column next to each SHP Preferred Sex Act.

When you look at this list, does it feel right to you? If not, *now* is the time to make adjustments. If you notice emotional lightness or a sense of relief and of excitement in your body, then the list is most likely right for you at this time.

Activation Scale

10
9
8
7
6
5
4
3
2
1

1.

2.

3.

4.

5.

6.

Congratulations, you've completed your Sexual Health Plan!

Somatic Notes

Facial Cues
(I notice tension in my jaw, around my lips, between my eyes, forehead, etc.)

Bodily Cues
(I notice tension in my arms, legs, chest, stomach, rectum, etc. I notice that I'm fidgeting, have shallow breathing, or I'm not breathing, have a dry mouth, etc.)

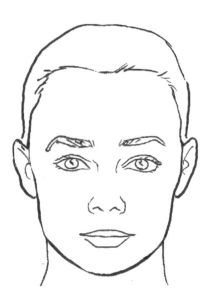
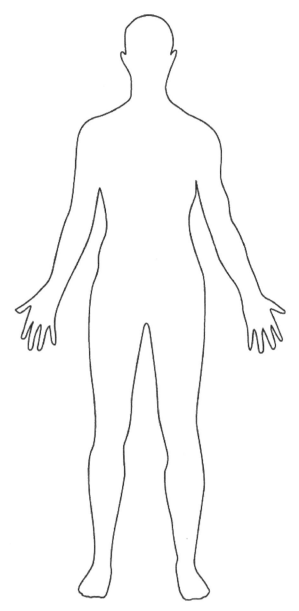

Homework

Vocal Cues
(I notice constriction in my throat, my voice seems different, my tone of voice is higher or lower, etc.)

_____
_____
_____
_____
_____
_____
_____

Behavioral Cues
(I'm having difficulty concentrating, etc.)

_____
_____
_____
_____
_____
_____
_____
_____

Color in the image on the following page. →

Then, write a story or poem about the image, or a memory it brings up for you. Remember to create a beginning and ending and to acknowledge any feelings the image evoked in you.

My Story / Poem / Memory

Reflections Log

Use this space between sessions to record any thoughts, feelings, images, memories or ideas that came to you as you completed this section.

Chapter 6

The Interpersonal-Intrapsychic Dimension of Sexuality

THERAPISTS:
See Appendix pages xi – xii

This phase of this process examines your interpersonal relationships and your internal processes related to your sexuality. As before, answer the questions as honestly as possible, and always use your activation level and bodily-based impulses as a compass guiding you to your truth.

I. Discussion for the partnered

How do you think your partner will respond to your Sexual Health Plan?
Your therapist will now take you through a guided meditation, so you can imagine what it would be like to discuss your SHP with your partner. Follow your therapist's instructions.

Now that the guided meditation is complete, recall any thoughts or feelings that arose during the process and report them to your therapist. Then ask yourself, "On a scale of 1 to 10, how comfortable do I feel now about discussing my SHP with my partner?" Notice where you feel any sensations in your body. Ask yourself, "What are my next steps?"

1. When will you request a conversation?

2. Using the Activation Scale, how vulnerable do you imagine you'll feel?

3. Where should the conversation take place?

4. How will you set the stage for the conversation?

5. What boundaries do you need to set to keep you both safe?

6. How might you talk about what you want and need sexually in a way that is non threatening or judging of your partner?

7. How will you respond to his or her reactions?

8. How will you handle "no" without violating your or his/her dignity?

9. Will you set another time to continue the conversation?

II. Dating Plan for the Single

If you are single and in recovery, constructing a dating plan is essential at this time so you can move towards having casual sex until you're ready for a relationship. This stage lets you practice your sexuality with another and keeps you out of a sexually anorexic rut. Take this time to consider what would work best for you.

Take a look at the suggested Recovery Dating Plan, on page 107, adapted from *Erotic Intelligence* (Katehakis, 2010) as a guideline. But as always, do what's right *for you*.

A Recovery Dating Plan should help you clarify how to choose a suitable partner, and then help you create a realistic timeline for healthy dating behavior. In the first section, you'll see a grid with three columns labeled Green, Yellow and Red. Green should represent your ideal qualities; yellow are warning signs that you should heed, and red are your deal-breakers.

The more work you put into delineating the qualities you want in another, the more useful your plan will be.

As with all of the work in this book, challenge yourself to dig deep when you ask yourself, "What qualities am I seeking in a partner?" Be as specific as you can when you imagine your ideal person. Then remember we're all human, so stay flexible about your ideals. When you're dating, consider the following questions (and feel free to add your own):

1. Does this person align with my personal values?

_____

_____

How do you know?

_____

_____

_____

_____

2. Am I giving him/her the benefit of the doubt?

_____

_____

_____

_____

_____

_____

_____

3. Are any of my old traumatic or addictive patterns (like bragging, overpaying, or avoiding my feelings) present in our interactions? (Name those tendencies now so you can be on the lookout for them.)

4. Do I over-share or hide out in order to manage my anxiety?

If so, why do you think that's happening?

5. Do I go into fantasy, regress emotionally, become defensive or aggressive?

If so, why do you think that's happening?

6. Am I using humor inappropriately or holding it back?

If so, why do you think that's happening?

7. Do I listen attentively to her/him and have an even exchange of ideas, or do I dominate the conversation or let her/him dominate the conversation?

If one of the latter is happening, why do you think that's happening?

8. Do I tend to violate my time boundaries by letting the date go on too long?

If so, why do you think that's happening?

Ideal Dating Qualities

GREEN (Ideal qualities)	YELLOW (Warning signs)	RED (Deal-breakers)
• Genuinely look forward to seeing the person • Tell the truth • Take an active interest and ask questions to get to know the person • Compliment from a solid place in myself, not out of need • Say "good night" in an appropriate way that feels good for me	• Overspend to impress my date • Obsess about what was said and examine every nuance • Find myself trying to "fix" the other person or his/her problems • Value the other's opinion or time more than my own • Fantasize about our future together • Rationalize not getting my needs met	• Miss work or meetings to be with the person • Lie about myself • Lie by omission • Become more isolated and my social circle is diminishing • Rationalize a lot of behaviors that have me out of my integrity • Find I'm not that interested in the person but go out anyway because I don't have any other prospects • Have sex because I haven't in a long time

Adapted and reprinted with permission from *Erotic Intelligence: Igniting Hot, Healthy Sex While in Recovery From Sex Addiction* (2010) HCI Publications.

Use the Activation Scale as you write your plan. By checking in with yourself that way, you'll see if you're on the right track. Remember, the body knows what's best!

After you've written your dating plan, read it to your therapist and others in recovery so you can get constructive, supportive feedback. Keep working on it until it feels right for you at this time. Remember, these plans are dynamic guidelines and meant to change as you deepen your recovery.

Dating Timeline

Dates 1–4 (1st month)

- Talk on the phone 1–2x / week max
- Text messages used sparingly
- Dating others
- No serious talk about your history or past relationships
- Hug, kiss on cheek
- Both take cars, meet there
- Spend < $100 on a date

Dates 5–8 (2 months)

- "Light" petting, above the waist (hands), outside clothes
- French kissing
- Talking on phone < 4x / week
- Text messages are not excessive
- Seeing each other's house/home
- Physical affection
- Spend > $100 on a date

Dates 9–15 (3 months)

- Discontinue dating others before having intercourse discussion
- Disclosure about sexual history and addiction (before intercourse!)
- Discussion about STIs and birth control
- Intercourse with condom only
- Oral sex
- Sleep over at each other's house
- Short vacations (i.e., weekends away)

Activation Scale

10
9
8
7
6
5
4
3
2
1

My Dating Plan

Somatic Notes

Facial Cues
(I notice tension in my jaw, around my lips, between my eyes, forehead, etc.)

Bodily Cues
(I notice tension in my arms, legs, chest, stomach, rectum, etc. I notice that I'm fidgeting, have shallow breathing, or I'm not breathing, have a dry mouth, etc.)

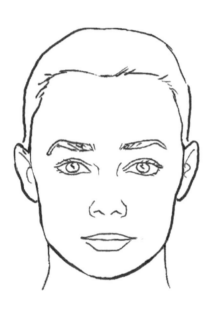
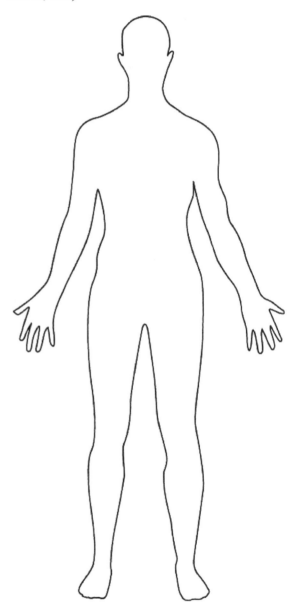

Vocal Cues
(I notice constriction in my throat, my voice seems different, my tone of voice is higher or lower, etc.)

_____

_____

_____

_____

_____

_____

_____

Behavioral Cues
(I'm having difficulty concentrating, etc.)

_____

_____

_____

_____

_____

_____

_____

Homework

Color in the image on the following page. →

Then, write a story or poem about the image, or a memory it brings up for you. Remember to create a beginning and ending and to acknowledge any feelings the image evoked in you.

My Story / Poem / Memory

Reflections Log

Use this space between sessions to record any thoughts, feelings, images, memories or ideas that came to you as you completed this section.

Chapter 7

The Spiritual Dimension of Sexuality

Spiritual or religious beliefs have meaning for some people and not for others. Regardless of your preferences, the ability to talk openly about the meaning of sex, spirituality and religion *for you* is an adult developmental skill. If you have any leftover sexual shame or guilt due to any abusive spiritual or religious beliefs, now is the time to process those feelings with your therapist.

Consider the questions below on the spiritual dimension of your sexuality. Read these questions and discuss them with your therapist:

Read the answers aloud to your therapist. Process any feelings or thoughts that arise. Use the Activation Scale to indicate how activated you are. Notice emotions evoked in your body and indicate those on the Somatic Notes, if helpful.

1. Have you made a conscious choice about your spiritual or religious preferences (including agnosticism or atheism) through a teacher, mentor, therapist, the 12-step program, or other means? If so, describe the beliefs you ascribe to in detail.

_____

_____

_____

_____

_____

_____

_____

_____

_____

_____

_____

_____

_____

_____

_____

2. Can you discuss your choices and beliefs with your partner?

3. Can you imagine your spiritual or religious beliefs adding to your sexual experience in a positive way? If so, how? If not, why not?

4. Can you imagine taking deliberate actions to set the stage for the kind of sexual/spiritual experience you want? If so, what would you do, and how would you do it? Be specific.

5. Can you imagine yourself remaining fluid during sex by making a meaningful connection between the spiritual and the sexual? How do you imagine making conscious contact with the divine, or a force or presence greater than yourself?

6. Are you willing to discover more of your personal truths by exploring the spiritual realm as well as your physical senses during sex? Would these be new explorations for you? If so how will you evoke the spiritual along with all of your senses? If not, how have you explored these arenas successfully in the past?

7. Are you ready to make yourself vulnerable by communicating and receiving communication about your and another's deepest thoughts and feelings before and during sex? Can you see how this would move you towards your full potential for intimacy and a long-term love relationship?

Activation Scale

10
9
8
7
6
5
4
3
2
1

Somatic Notes

Facial Cues
(I notice tension in my jaw, around my lips, between my eyes, forehead, etc.)

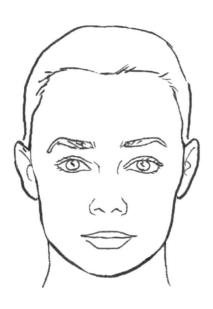

Bodily Cues
(I notice tension in my arms, legs, chest, stomach, rectum, etc. I notice that I'm fidgeting, have shallow breathing, or I'm not breathing, have a dry mouth, etc.)

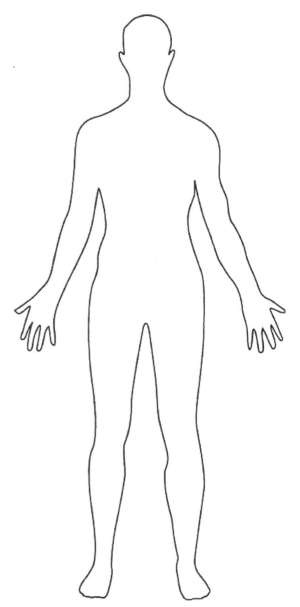

Vocal Cues
(I notice constriction in my throat, my voice seems different, my tone of voice is higher or lower, etc.)

_____
_____
_____
_____
_____
_____
_____

Behavioral Cues
(I'm having difficulty concentrating, etc.)

_____
_____
_____
_____
_____
_____
_____
_____

Homework

Color in the image on the following page. →

Then, write a story or poem about the image, or a memory it brings up for you. Remember to create a beginning and ending and to acknowledge any feelings the image evoked in you.

My Story / Poem / Memory

Reflections Log

Use this space between sessions to record any thoughts, feelings, images, memories or ideas that came to you as you completed this section.

Your Sexual Health Checklist

Check the following boxes to verify that you've reached your goal of bringing optimal sexuality, in all five of its dimensions, into your life. If a box is left unchecked, go back and revisit the sections you feel would most support you in strengthening those areas. If necessary, answer the questions in that section again and process the section with your therapist.

1. Physical Dimension

☐ You can distinguish sexual behaviors that are harmful or exploitative to yourself or to another from sexual behaviors that bring dignity, vitality, and pleasure to yourself and to another

☐ You are aware of your sexual response cycle, and enjoy satisfactory physical responsiveness based on optimal functioning in your brain/body/mind.

☐ You understand your sexual body (anatomy, physiology, sexual dysfunction and related needs), and have gotten tested for STIs and other physical risks.

2. Affective Dimension

☐ You don't feel guilty or shameful about sex and sexual behavior and you don't reenact previous trauma that induces dissociative feelings (loss of or distancing from yourself).

☐ You can track and name the impulses in your body as feelings, and can trust these impulses as a personal guide to what feels right and what feels wrong to you.

☐ You can communicate and receive communication about thoughts and feelings, and possess the potential for intimacy, vulnerability, and a long-term love relationship.

☐ You are excited about sex and feel that pleasurable sexual acts restore your sense of dignity and worth.

3. Cognitive Dimension

☐ You can relate to a lover with appropriate boundaries: Specifically, you know when to say "no;" can hear "no" from another; don't violate your dignity or body by engaging in unwanted sexual experiences; and don't take sexual advantage of another through physical or psychological manipulation.

☐ If you're single, you have constructed a dating plan and a sexual plan; if you're in a relationship, you have constructed a sexual plan.

☐ You can take deliberate actions to set the stage for the kind of sexual experience you want.

4. Interpersonal-Intrapsychic Dimension

☐ You have comfortably talked with a partner about a range of preferred sexual experiences and have disclosed to a partner your health status (HIV, STI, activity in or recovery from sex addiction, alcoholism, gambling or other addictions).

☐ You report comfort with a range of preferred sexual experiences, including masturbation, and you can discuss them with a partner, friend, potential love interest, and therapist without shame.

☐ You experience and can report to your therapist openness to discovering your personal truth via the senses during sex.

☐ You have a felt sense in your body that sexual preferences and choices are congruent with your gender identity.

5. Spiritual Dimension

☐ You have made a conscious choice about your spiritual or religious preferences (including agnosticism or atheism) through your chosen avenues (12-step program, teacher, mentor, clergy person or therapist), and you can discuss your choices with your therapist and your partner.

☐ Spiritual or religious beliefs enrich your sexual experience rather than visit shame or guilt on you.

☐ You remain fluid during sex, can make a meaningful connection between the spiritual and the sexual, and can choose to process spiritual/sexual experiences with another to understand and deepen your sexual/spiritual life.

Farewell

For many, sex has been a source of shame and a compulsion that contradicted personal ethical and sexual values. It was devoid of spiritual meaning, dismissive of others, and dissociated from their very sense of self.

For you, as for many others, there came a time when it became imperative to distinguish between sexual behaviors that felt destructive and those that felt exalting and life-affirming. No longer operating from a traumatized or immature place, you recognized that being compulsively driven toward immediate, non-relational, sometimes shameful pleasure revealed that genuine, intentional, joyous sexuality was lacking within. And you courageously undertook to liberate or to create it.

Before you began this Workbook, you realized that the fun fantasy of endless, mindless sex has been painful in actual practice. In completing the Workbook, you found that moralistic repression and reckless impulsivity are flip sides of the same coin. Instead of either, self-awareness and moderation helped you hone your sexual desires and put them in their rightful place—as expressions of your truest, best self. You saw that giving and receiving pleasure generously and making sex a priority in your relationship both kept it fresh and prevented it from luring you into violating your values. You learned that when sexual pleasure is restored to its rightful place—in the conscious foreground of your life—it can be the force that allows your life and relationship to flourish.

This new perspective on sex lets you start to forge a personal healthy sexuality that's deeply satisfying and, over time, will enrich the whole landscape of your life with meaning. These two components—bodily pleasure and emotional significance—are central in the experience of sexual health.

You also found that recovery from any injury takes commitment, discipline, perseverance, and sheer guts. Your having put in the time and energy to complete this Workbook is a sure sign that you have taken the leap toward reclaiming your rightful, healthy sexuality.

With your new Sexual Health Plan, I hope that you venture into the world of sexual pleasure and the erotic with a newfound sense of your self, and that you celebrate *your* healthy sexuality.

May you love well!

— Alexandra Katehakis

Additional Notes

Chapter 1

Psychobiological Approach to Sex Addiction Treatment (PASAT) Guide

THERAPIST ANNOTATIONS

This workbook relies on the Psychobiological Approach to Sex Addiction Treatment (PASAT) Guide to help you discover what's true for your client. It may take a session or two to read through this guide together, but don't skip this process or your results will fall short.

PASAT centers on the relationship between you and your client and the felt experiences you will have shared. You'll often ask your client to notice the feelings, impulses and sensations in their body, record or reflect on them using worksheets, and discuss them in session. This way of working familiarizes the client with how their nervous system responds to a stimulus. By getting to know their body/mind in this way, they'll learn more accurately what feels sexually healthy and pleasurable to them, and what doesn't. This process will also help the client become less compartmentalized about their sexuality–less cut-off from their self when they think about or have sex. In other words, there's no place for secrets about their sexual preferences in this work, only honesty about what brings them sexual fulfillment and how you can assist your client in making those acts part of their sexual life.

The user-friendly PASAT guide will help you track the inner landscape of your clients' body/mind. Its steps are: Tracking, Tracking Gestures, Bodily-Based Transference and Countertransference, Titration, Completion of the Response, Resources, Present Awareness, Regulation of Dorsal Motor Vagal Responses, Pendulation, and Finishing.

I. Tracking

Tracking means paying close attention to sensations and impulses in your client's body. Help them get into the habit of tracking their bodily-based sensations as they arise while the two of you talk about workbook assignments and about other issues during sessions. You should also be tracking the physiological changes you see in the client and asking about them.

Invite the client to give words, without too much thinking, to the sensations and impulses in her or his body. You may ask a body part to "speak," and suggest that the client just jump in and say whatever comes to mind. Encourage clients to use descriptors that emerge in the moment, such as colors or an image that captures their inner experience ("My heart feels black" or "I feel butterflies in my stomach"). You may ask your client to narrate his or her shifting internal experiences, without judgment, as they occur. For example, if the client says, "I feel stuck," you may ask, "Where are you feeling stuck in your body?" Remind clients to do the best they can to answer from their body and not their mind.

Your task is to raise the client's awareness of his or her gestures or movements. These nonverbal communications range from expressions of anger (such as clenched fists) to self-soothing ones (such as a hand on the chest) that serve to reduce dysegulated affect. Asking about these gestures gently brings your client's awareness into the present moment.

II. Tracking Gestures (therapist information)

Tracking gestures means bringing awareness to the natural gestures or movements of the client's body, as previously described. For example, the client may repeatedly but gently slide the top of her left hand along the top of her thigh. This indicates a right-brain process, since the brain/body is a contra-lateral system.

The therapist should gently notice and bring these movements into the client's present awareness. The therapist should also notice whether the gestures unconsciously mirror the therapist's own movements, as such echo behavior signals attunement. Conversely, the therapist may choose to mirror the client's behavior deliberately in order to amplify it, then ask the client what the gesture is "saying." Ask the client to repeat the movement as long as needed until she or he can give it a "voice."

III. Somatic Countertransference

Somatic countertransference refers to the nonverbal, body-to-body conversation taking place within the dyad and which the therapist experiences as sensations or impulses in his or her body.

It is now generally accepted that the deep unconscious resides in the body and that the unconscious is at play at all times. Therefore, the therapist should constantly notice impulses arising in his or her own body and use that information when appropriate. The therapist's high level of attunement to the self simultaneously helps bring the implicit (unconscious) experience of the client into the client's explicit (conscious) awareness.

There will undoubtedly be times when the client begins to notice feelings toward you as you negotiate the nooks and crannies of his or her sexual psyche. The client may feel frustrated, embarrassed, or even sexually attracted to you, regardless of sexual orientation. These are normal feelings of *transference* whereby the client transfers or infuses her or his feelings into you. It's natural that you might become the object of the client's anger, or the object of his or her sexual fantasy because they're talking about sex and sexuality with you. Common, healthy, and beneficial in therapy, this experience is best utilized by talking about it. Whatever feelings come up for clients in therapeutic work can help them clarify who they are sexually, so remind them to take risks by being rigorously honest.

Throughout this process, you should also be judiciously reporting your experience of what it feels like to be in your client's presence (*countertransference*). Track the impulses in your body, and tell the client what you are noticing when the information would be helpful to him or her.

For example, if the client reports feeling "blank," the therapist should notice what he or she is feeling in his or her own body. The therapist may respond by saying something like, "I, too, am noticing a blankness in the middle of my body." This statement lets the client feel felt and experienced by the therapist and, thus, deeply known. Another possibility may occur when the client is feeling "vacant, numb" or "nothing." At these times, the therapist may feel and be able to identify anger in his or her chest, nausea in the gut, or a myriad of other emotions being transferred somatically. Being exquisitely aware and conversant with their own bodily-based cues is crucial to therapists' ability to track their own and their clients' affective states.

Even in casual conversation, people often verbalize their bodily feelings in the presence of others. The difference now is that you and your client will talk about these sensations in a way that increases the client's ability to see himself or herself and to be seen, known, and understood by another.

IV. Titration

Titration refers to a process of gradually exploring the sensations in the body. It allows clients to slow down so they can internally "read" their emergent bodily cues. Since pathological dissociation results from a disconnection between the cortical and subcortical parts of the brain and an uncoupling of circuits, graduated exposure to the emotions in the body—what neuropsychoanalyst Allan Schore describes as "affectively tolerable doses" invites neural integration without overwhelming the system. Clients should be instructed to "simply notice, without judgment what the felt sense in the body is, then express it the best they can.

Questions to guide the client into bodily sensations:
"Where are you noticing the sensation in your body?"
"Does the sensation have a size or shape?"
"Does it have a weight?"
"Does it have a color?"
"Does it have a temperature?"
"What happens internally as you put your attention on any part of it?"
"Can you dive into the sensation, size, shape, or feeling?"
"If not, what stops you? Notice the block and honor it." (Explore the block, repeating questions-6.)

If no block is reported, ask the client, "What happens if you exaggerate the feeling?"
"What happens if you diminish the feeling?"
"If the feeling could speak, what would it say it needs or wants?"

V. Completion of the Response

When affective/somatic processes are "alive," the body comes alive. The therapist must track bodily movements and impulses to assist the client in *completing* the action he or she couldn't when under siege in childhood.

Questions to guide the client into active response when sympathetic arousal (fight/flight) is evident:
"Where would you say the center of energy is in your body?"
"Does your body want to move in any particular way? If so, can you express that movement? (You can mirror the client's movement to help amplify it, but don't get ahead of the client by exaggerating the movement; ask the client to do that. The act of making the movement with the client often gives her or him permission to amplify it independently.) Encourage the client to get up and walk in the space if he or she wants to move in a particular way.
"Is there a sound the sensation(s) in your body would like to make?" (You can echo the client's sound to help amplify it but, again, don't get ahead of the client by getting too loud; the act of making the sound with the client often gives permission to her or him to amplify it independently.)
"Is there anything you need at this time, in this state of being?"
"What's missing for you?"

THERAPIST ANNOTATIONS

Questions to guide the client into active response when a dorsal motor vagal response (freeze) is evident:

"Do you notice any numbness, vacancy or emptiness in your body?"

"Can you dive into the nothingness and see what's there?"

"What happens when you become the nothingness?"

"If the nothingness could make even the slightest move, what might it do?"

"What effect does that have on you?"

"If the nothingness could speak, what small sound would it make?"

"Is there anything you need in this moment?" (The client may answer, "Help.")

"Can you ask for what you need now, in this state of being?" (This asks the client to make an "I" statement such as, "I need help.")

"What's missing for you?"

VI. Resources

There will be times when the client reaches the regulatory boundaries of his or her window of tolerance.

Whether at the regulatory boundaries of hyperarousal or hypoarousal, he or she can use a positive or neutral memory image to restore his or her functioning to a ventral vagal state of good heart-rate variability.

The most effective way to use resourcing is to allow the client to focus on his or her interoceptive cues. Ask the client to name the impulses or sensations in her or his body that are most dysregulating (such as fear, sadness, pain), then ask her or him to shift focus from the disturbing affective state to the imagined resource (similar to shifting from an "incomplete target" in EMDR to a "safe place").

Sensations associated with sympathetic hyperarousal are tachycardia (rapid heartbeat), sweaty palms, muscle tension, shaking of extremities, rapid breathing (hyperventilation), and distended eyeballs (eyes appear unnaturally open).

Sensations associated with parasympathetic hypoarousal are bradycardia (slow heartbeat), lack of muscle tone, limp extremities, and stilling of autonomic nervous system resulting in holding of breath, downcast eyes, and limp neck.

Sensations associated with ventral vagal tone are full-body breathing into the gut, regular heartbeat, good muscle tone, relaxed muscles, and an active social engagement system (ability to smile, laugh, socially engage in a grounded, calm way).

Sensations associated with the release of traumatic energy are shaking, trembling, yawning, sensations of warmth in the body, burping, laughter, tears, and any general movement of energy (including improved digestion).

By calling on this type of simple *resource*, the client should be able to bring forth a regulated or preferred physical state.

A resource can be, but is not limited to, a calming memory or image such as:

– A safe place (perhaps one has already been installed from EMDR; check with the client prior to engaging in this process)

– A safe container where bad feelings or people can be deposited (another EMDR resource; check with the client prior to engaging in this process to see if this has previously been established)

– An experience in which the client was able to find comfort and connection with another or with the environment

– A secure or calming other (grandparent, mystical teacher, pet, transitional object)

– A life experience wherein the client was the victor (escaping a difficult situation, accomplishing a physical, emotional, or mental feat she or he thought was impossible)

VII. Present Awareness

Present awareness means being fully in the moment with the client. A safe, non-judgmental, focused presence is telegraphed through the therapist's spontaneous facial expressions, eye contact, gestures, and prosody. These all serve to assist the client's movement toward neural integration.

Present awareness includes an invitation to ground or connect deeply to the earth by asking clients to notice their feet on the floor, the weight of their body on the furniture, the objects in the environment, and any other sights outside a window or outside of oneself, or smells that bring them into the present field. Soft, non-threatening eye contact within the therapeutic dyad can also be grounding for some.

VIII. Regulation of Dorsal Motor Vagal Responses

If the client begins to experience perceptual disturbances such as dry mouth, ringing of ears, spots before their eyes or feeling faint, he or she is moving towards a *dorsal motor vagal* state of collapse. In this instance, it is crucial to assist the client in returning to a ventral vagal state of good heart-rate variability.

The therapist should employ any of these simple directives as soon as such extreme affect dysregulation is observed in the client. Below are some simple options you can ask the client to do:

1. Look around the room and name the various shapes

2. Name various colors

3. Name various items

4. Shake off the traumatic sensations by shaking the entire body; the therapist should guide the shaking and do it with the client

5. Stand up and walk around the room

6. Notice the temperature in the room

7. Ask the client to push her or his hands against a door or wall, activating the arms and legs

8. If the client can't stand up, place a pillow between both of your hands and ask the client to activate his or her arms to assist their nervous system in becoming more regulated. Instruct the client to push against the pillow while you push back with similar pressure. There should be a firm pressing motion between the two of you.

9. Take a drink of water

10. Breathe into the chest to assist in activating the system

On occasion, clients may become hyper-aroused and unable to down-regulate the arousal state. If so, instruct them to do any of the following:

– Grab a pillow and hold it tightly to their chest

– Use the EMDR butterfly tap for bi-lateral stimulation while thinking about a safe place to calm themselves

– Breathe into their belly

– Use one of their resources

IX. Pendulation

Pendulation is a technique used in Somatic Experiencing© and other well-established somatic modalities. It assists the autonomic nervous system (ANS) to become more flexible over time. When clients are badly traumatized as infants or children, their ANS becomes primed to distress. Pendulation gently restores the ANS to a more flexible rhythm so that the natural functions of sympathetic and parasympathetic arousal are in concert with each other.

This is best practiced by moving the client from a regulated, alert, calm state of being to a moderately activated state of being and then back again. The exercise helps the ANS to recalibrate and return to its natural functioning. For example, after you have resourced your client, you may direct him or her to bring up a memory that is activating. Ask him or her to notice bodily impulses and sensations and to track their somatic cues while doing so. In short order, direct the client to one of his or her resources, all the while tracking his or her breathing, skin conductance, tonicity in the body, and so forth. When the client returns to a ventral vagal state, pendulate him or her back to the arousal state, then repeat.

X. Finishing

It is important to bring every session to a close and for the client to experience and to assert that he or she is *finished*. Check in with the client:

– Ask, "What do you notice now about the overall state of your body?" (There can be a wide array of thoughts, feelings, and sensations. Look for signs of the social engagement system being back online: smiles, laughter, eye contact, normal breathing, and relaxed facial muscles

– Have the client state aloud, "I'm finished."

A session will be unfinished if the client reports feeling distressed or if you observe signs of affect dysregulation. Below are some things you can do to bring your client back to a regulated state:

– Take a moment to ground the client through the use of one of her or his resources

– Use the pendulation processes at this time

– Remind clients to simply notice "what is" and not to judge, fix, or struggle to change their state of being. Assure them that the body will adjust accordingly, and remind them that they can use their resources outside of your office

– Suggest the client take a walk around the block before getting into their car and driving. Remind them to stay in present awareness on the walk; this is essentially a walking meditation. Guide them to notice their feet on the ground, the air on their face, the sunshine on their body, the sights and smells, and to bring their wandering mind back to pure, present awareness

– Assure the client that "this, too, shall pass." Remind them that they're on the road to healing because they're beginning to feel their feelings, no longer in a numb, "dead" or dissociated state

– Suggest they may bring an actual resource (stuffed animal, photo, trinket) with them to the next session

– Remind the client that she or he may call you between sessions if needed

THERAPIST NOTATIONS

Chapter 5

THERAPIST ANNOTATIONS

**V. Preferred Sex Acts
or a Repetition of Your Trauma?**

Therapist instructions for specific questions Section V, page 74: When a client finds pleasurable the thought or actuality of a sex act that is not based in his or her trauma, yet they have negative judgment about it, now is the time to work on shame reduction.

Another client may find a sexual act or scenario pleasurable that occurred during a traumatic sexual experience. If that client has done significant work around the trauma using a somatic modality (such as EMDR, Brainspotting or SE) and has greatly reduced dissociative features that accompany the act, that sex act or scenario should be normalized.

It's important to stay in a collaborative conversation with the client to advance his or her clarity about what's most appropriate for him or her at this time.

These guiding questions will assist you in this process:
   "What specifically about the sex act feels shaming to you?"
   "Where did you get the idea that this sex act was something you shouldn't engage in? Do you agree with this?"
   "What would it say about you if you engaged in this sex act?"
   "Is it possible that you could feel shame during sex and be aroused by that feeling of shame? Do you know that shame/humiliation dynamics often play out in consensual sex such as BDSM practices and various role-plays, and that some people find those dynamics arousing? Is this true for you? Do you feel shame about liking to be shamed sexually?"
   "If you are aroused by shame dynamics during sex, can you talk to your partner about it?"
   "If you are aroused by shame dynamics during sex, do you think you can feel dignified and 'okay' about yourself after sex, or will you collapse into toxic shame and be triggered to act out sexually?"
   "If we can't come to a conclusion about this particular sex act, can we put it on a 'Watch and Wait' list and continue talking about it over time?"
   "What do you know about the 'Watch and Wait' strategy? How do you feel about the 'Watch and Wait' strategy?"

Finally, ask the client, "How activated are you by this conversation?"

Direct the client to the Activation Scale and to their somatic cues, then have them note under Section V whether shame has diminished or increased regarding their preferred sex acts. Ask them to re-scale each one for comparison purposes.

Note: A couples guide is outside the purview of this model. It is up to you to discern when a couple is ready for these conversations and whether you need to recommend books, refer them out, or refer them to a couples intensive workshop or program.

THERAPIST NOTATIONS

Chapter 6

THERAPIST ANNOTATIONS

Guided Meditation — Therapist Script

Begin by placing both feet on the floor, sitting comfortably in your seat and gently closing your eyes. Take a deep breath into your belly, then exhale, and again, a deep breath, expanding the belly, then exhaling through the nose, and one last time, filling the belly and exhaling through the nose. Now let your breathing settle into a normal pattern. Let yourself notice any sensations in the body by gently putting your attention on them. Whether tightness, emptiness, tension, or relaxation—don't judge the feelings, just notice them with simple attention. Likewise, notice any sounds in your surroundings without judgment, then gently bring your attention back to your body.

Notice how you feel when you think about talking to your partner about your preferred sex acts. Gently pay attention to where in your body you notice sensations, impulses, or emptiness. Gently breathe into any areas of tension, tightness, emptiness, or numbness. Rest your attention on any sensations that feel pleasurable or neutral in this moment. The task is to simply notice, without judgment, what's happening in your body.

Imagine the setting you would like to be in when you talk to your partner. Choose a place that feels safe and secure for you both.

Notice the sights, sounds, and smells of your surroundings. What do you need to feel safe and centered? Can you imagine experiencing that safety and security when you have this conversation?

See your partner in a receptive mode. Where is (she/he) sitting? How does (she/he) look?

See yourself sitting opposite (him/her), knee to knee and making eye contact. What do you see?

Imagine talking about your sexual preferences to your partner without shame, and see your partner listening like a good friend. What do you notice now in your partner? In yourself?

Imagine a positive outcome, whether you get what you want or not. What would a positive outcome look and feel like between the two of you? How would you leave this conversation? Can you imagine setting another time to revisit the conversation?

How do you feel when the conversation is over? See the conversation ending at a natural stopping point and saying, "Thank you" to your partner for (his/her) presence and willingness. Then see the two of you parting ways peacefully.

THERAPIST NOTATIONS

THERAPIST NOTATIONS

About the Author

Alexandra Katehakis, Ph.D., LMFT is the Founder of Center for Healthy Sex in Los Angeles. She is a Clinical Sexologist, Certified Sex Addiction Therapist/Supervisor and AASECT Certified Sex Therapist/Supervisor specializing in human sexuality. Dr. Katehakis is faculty for the International Institute of Trauma and Addiction Professionals, and the 2012 Carnes Award recipient. She is author of *Sex Addiction As Affect Dysregulation: A Neurobiologically Informed Holistic Treatment* (2016), co-author of the award winning *Mirror of Intimacy: Daily Reflections on Emotional and Erotic Intelligence* (2014), contributing author to *Making Advances: A Comprehensive Guide for Treating Female Sex and Love Addicts,* M. Ferree (Ed.), (2012), and author of *Erotic Intelligence: Igniting Hot Healthy Sex While in Recovery From Sex Addiction* (2010).

Made in United States
Troutdale, OR
08/23/2023

12290097R00084